Journey Five

A collection of images from Travel Photographer of the Year

D1381590

Travel Photographer of the Year Ltd - The Photographers' Press

Publisher/Editor/Author - Chris Coe
Editor - Karen Coe
Sub Editors - Emma Thomson & Justine Wheeler
Designer - Gabrielle Davies

First published by Travel Photographer of the Year Ltd,
20 Yew Tree Courtyard, Earl Soham, Suffolk IP13 7SG, UK
www.tpoty.com

First edition published in July 2013
ISBN 13: 978-0-9549396-5-6

Reproduced, printed and bound by Connekt Colour Berkhamstead, HP4 1EH, UK

Front cover photograph: Dhaka, Bangladesh. **Jonathan Munshi, USA.**

Frontispiece photograph: Cloudbreak, Fiji. **Chris McLellan, New Zealand.**

Page 3 photograph: Havana, Cuba. **Jeremy Woodhouse, UK.**

Page 5 photograph: Snow Hill Island, Antarctica. **Geoff Edwards, UK.**

Back cover photograph (top): Omo River Valley, Ethiopia. **Jan Schlegel, Germany.**

Back cover photograph (middle): Siberia, Russia. **Alessandra Meniconzi, Switzerland.**

Back cover photograph (bottom): Namib desert, Namibia. **Marsel van Oosten, Netherlands.**

CONTENTS

It's been an incredible ten-year journey to get to this point and, as Travel Photographer of the Year celebrates its first decade, a new adventure begins with Journey Five. Our prized books will now be published annually in a smaller, lighter format, but to the same high quality to make the photographs really sing.

This fifth collection of images is again inspired by light and the craft of the photographers who enter the awards. As always, this latest travelogue takes us to the four corners of the planet, capturing life, beauty, harsh reality, human endeavour, nature's majesty and the spirit of Planet Earth. It takes the best elements from Journeys One, Two, Three and Four, but is also refreshingly different.

In the last decade, photography has witnessed dramatic changes. In the early days of the awards, digital photography was in its infancy and film was still king. Award entries were all on prints. Now almost all are shot digitally and uploaded, the original buried on a hard drive somewhere. What's more, the sheer volume of images we're exposed to on a daily basis is truly phenomenal. Naturally volume and quality are wholly different but it does pose a greater challenge to photographers to find originality and a new creative view of our life and our planet, so that it stands out amongst the plethora of mediocre imagery that is shot daily.

It's a challenge that photographers rise to though, and Journey Five bears witness to this with some truly outstanding imagery. Producing these books, along with the Travel Photographer of the Year exhibitions, is one of life's joys. Despite living in an increasingly digital and internet-driven world, images only truly sing when they are displayed on the printed page or as a professionally printed image in a gallery. Only these forms of media make great photographs come alive.

As the technology improves it is refreshing to see a growing awareness that, for all the bells and whistles on the latest cameras, photography is, and always will be, about seeing, about light, about time and about composition. It is easy to believe that an expensive camera equals great images, but it's a mistake that many of us make on our photographic journeys. Seeing takes time, and one of the best things about photography is that it demands our time; it makes us slow down, it makes us observe and it makes us appreciate surroundings that modern life often makes us take for granted.

Journey Five is waiting for you to turn the page. It's waiting for you to take the first step of a new journey. As you look and read, you will be transported to both familiar and unfamiliar places. Be prepared for your wanderlust to be stirred. Perhaps this book should come with a warning, because by the time you reach the closing shot you'll almost certainly want to book your next holiday or start a new adventure!

The most amazing thing is that the pictures were made by people like you. Sure, some are taken by professional photographers, but many are taken by accountants, writers, secretaries, CEOs, marketeers - ordinary people with common passions for travel and photography. Perhaps it is for this reason that the

photographs are so engaging, accessible and fascinating. Most inspiring of all, are the images by the young photographers. The youngest in this book is just ten years old and all are creating images accomplished beyond their years. The future's bright!

Savour images of mid-west American cowboys, proud Ethiopian warriors, Arctic wildlife and majestic African-night skies, but travel needn't always involve distant lands. Inspiration can be found closer to home too. The Scottish islands - renowned for their changeable weather - feature strongly in this volume. A resourceful photographer uses these unique moments of light and shade to create intriguing, enchanting and everlasting images.

Whether you read Journey Five from cover to cover, or simply dive into random pages, remember to immerse yourself in the images; appreciate the vision and skill of the photographers. You will, of course, have your favourites but some are also a slow burn - growing on you and intriguing you more over time.

It's time for that first step! A new journey begins...

TRAVEL PHOTOGRAPHER OF THE YEAR 2012

The Cutty Sark Award

Two vastly contrasting portfolios won Craig Easton the overall award. Sunshine and blue skies are all well and good if you want a suntan, but for photographers, changing light is much more interesting. In Scotland, when the skies are grey, breaks in the cloud shoot momentary shafts of light onto the landscape below and these have been beautifully captured. The shots of Paris have a more fun feel to them and the use of monochrome gives them much more impact.

Sponsors of this award:

Cutty Sark Blended Scotch Whisky

The Minch, Western Isles, Scotland. **Craig Easton, UK.** *Nikon D3X with 70mm lens; f4; 1/320s; ISO 100.*

The Minch, Western Isles, Scotland. **Craig Easton, UK.** *Nikon D3X with 200mm lens; f5; 1/200s; ISO 100.*

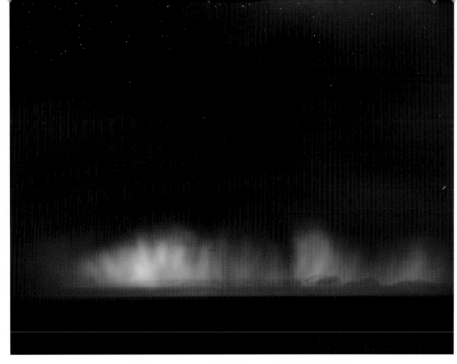

Trotternish, Isle of Skye, Scotland. **Craig Easton, UK.** *Nikon D3X with 150mm lens; f5; 1/200s; ISO 100.*

TRAVEL PHOTOGRAPHER
OF THE YEAR 2012

Craig Easton UK
Winner
The Cutty Sark Award

'Dreich' is an old Scottish word that describes dank, miserable weather. It seemed to me that there was often a beauty in those conditions that was not celebrated, so I started to go out with the camera looking for them. These pictures of a rainstorm passing along the Minch were shot from the Isle of Skye looking out towards the outer Hebrides. Keeping the cameras clean and dry was one of the hardest parts, as well as holding onto them in the wind. The light was extraordinary though and well worth getting soaked for.

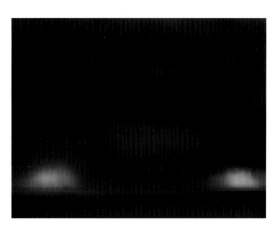

The Minch, Western Isles, Scotland. **Craig Easton, UK.**
Nikon D3X with 200mm lens; f5; 1/200s; ISO 100.

Paris, France. **Craig Easton, UK.** *Nikon D3X with 180mm lens; f5; 1/1600s; ISO 100.*

Paris, France. **Craig Easton, UK.** *Nikon D3X with 110mm lens; f7.1; 1/500s; ISO 100.*

Paris, France. **Craig Easton, UK.** *Nikon D3X with 110mm lens; f7.1; 1/500s; ISO 100.*

TRAVEL PHOTOGRAPHER
OF THE YEAR 2012

Craig Easton UK
Winner
The Cutty Sark Award

These pictures were taken on assignment for Fine Art materials company, Conté à Paris, as part of a series to evoke 'classic Paris' – images from the series are used on the packaging for their various sets of sketching pencils, pastels, and charcoals. The brief (unbelievably) was to walk the streets of Paris for four days shooting black-and-white reportage. I also had to tie in the subject matter loosely to the contents of each package, so I shot very graphic, architectural images for the sketching-pencil packs; fountains for the fixer spray cans; high-key white images for the chalks; and dark black night shots for the charcoals, etc. French privacy laws now dictate that I had to ensure no-one was recognisable in the images, which led me to the idea of silhouettes against an iconic background. Buildings can also present copyright issues, but in this case the Eiffel Tower is not protected by copyright law so I was OK. Had I shot it at night, however, it would have been another matter: the lighting on the tower is protected and you need a permit to use images of the Eiffel Tower lit up at night!

Paris, France. **Craig Easton, UK.** *Nikon D3X with 110mm lens; f7.1; 1/500s; ISO 100.*

YOUNG TRAVEL PHOTOGRAPHER OF THE YEAR 2012

Places & Faces: The quality of the images submitted for this category seems to rise every year and it is a source of great pleasure that young photographers are so inspired by the awards. At just 15 years of age, Samuel Fisch has produced images which are remarkably accomplished and elegantly capture a real sense of atmosphere.

Sponsors of this award:

Fujifilm, Adobe, Photo Iconic, Young Photographers' Alliance

Jackson Hole, Wyoming, USA. **Samuel Fisch, USA (age 15).** *Nikon D7000 with 70-200mm lens; f7.1; 1/800s; ISO 250.*

Jackson Hole, Wyoming, USA. **Samuel Fisch, USA (age 15).** *Nikon D7000 with 70-200mm lens; f5.6; 1/250s; ISO 500.*

YOUNG TRAVEL PHOTOGRAPHER OF THE YEAR 2012

Samuel Fisch USA
Winner

Last August we took a family trip to Grand Teton National Park and Yellowstone National Park. Each day, we passed a large group of horses. The light was very harsh during the day, so I returned to photograph the horses at sunrise, when I knew the light would be softer. As the sun appeared above the horizon, a group of cowboys began corralling the horses. I waited for one of them to start swinging his rope, as I knew the movement would add another element of interest to the shot. Once the cowboys finished corralling all of the horses, the dirt kicked up by the animals formed a tremendous dust cloud. The sun's rays pierced through the haze creating multiple silhouettes of the horses and cowboys. I was particularly drawn to the shadows and sunbeams around the horses' legs and the manner in which the sun illuminated their tails.

Jackson Hole, Wyoming, USA. **Samuel Fisch, USA (age 15).** *Nikon D7000 with 70-200mm lens; f2.8; 1/250s; ISO 250.*

Jackson Hole, Wyoming, USA. **Samuel Fisch, USA (age 15).** *Nikon D7000 with 70-200mm lens; f6.3; 1/1250s; ISO 1000.*

Kilgoris, Trans Mara, Rift Valley Province, Kenya. **Matthew Gillooley, USA (age 18).** *Nikon D700 with 24-70mm lens; f2.8; 1/800s; ISO 200.*

YOUNG TRAVEL PHOTOGRAPHER OF THE YEAR 2012

Matthew Gillooley USA
Winner - 15-18 age group

Left. A young boy protects his family's cows with his machete. When he saw his face on the LCD screen, he instantly smiled.

Opposite page. Two young students play football while barefoot with a ball made of trash bound together by twine. The child on the left has a bandage made of a trash bag on his right big toe.

Kilgoris, Trans Mara, Rift Valley Province, Kenya. **Matthew Gillooley, USA (age 18).**
Nikon D700 with 24-70mm lens; f2.8; 1/1250s; ISO 400.

YOUNG TRAVEL PHOTOGRAPHER OF THE YEAR 2012

Felicia Simion Romania
Runner Up - 15-18 age group

Below left. The woman who has as many smiles to give as wrinkles.

Below. A tale of love between the earth and skies.

Ciocăneşti, Dolj county, Romania. **Felicia Simion, Romania (age 18).**
Canon EOS 7D with 60mm lens; f2.8; 1/250s; ISO 200.

Bumbeşti Jiu, Gorj county, Romania. **Felicia Simion, Romania (age 18).** *Canon EOS 7D with 28-135mm lens; f3.5; 1/200s; ISO 125.*

YOUNG TRAVEL PHOTOGRAPHER OF THE YEAR 2012

Michael Theodric Indonesia
Winner - under 14 age group

Right. We hired this raftman to take us around the lake.

Opposite page. A fisherman casts his net early in the morning, with a beautiful mountain in the background.

Bagendit Lake, Situ Bagendit village, Garut, Indonesia. **Michael Theodric, Indonesia (age 10).**
Canon EOS5D Mark II with 17-40mm lens; f9; 1/1000s; ISO 400.

Bagendit Lake, Situ Bagendit village, Garut, Indonesia. **Michael Theodric, Indonesia (age 10).**
Canon EOS5D Mark II with 17-40mm lens; f8; 1/1000s; ISO 400.

Lalibela, Ethiopia. **Rebecca Deckmyn, Belgium (age 13).**
Panasonic Lumix DMCTZ10 with fixed 55mm lens; f3.9; 1/8s; ISO 400.

YOUNG TRAVEL PHOTOGRAPHER OF THE YEAR 2012

Rebecca Deckmyn Belgium
Runner Up - under 14 age group

Top right, bottom right. Reading the Bible
during Easter week.

Lalibela, Ethiopia. **Rebecca Deckmyn, Belgium (age 13).**
Panasonic Lumix DMCTZ10 with fixed 44mm lens; f3.7; 1/60s; ISO 125.

Austrian Alps. **Mateusz Piesiak, Poland (age 16).** *Canon 90D with Sigma 17-70mm lens; f3.2; 30s; ISO 800.*

YOUNG TRAVEL PHOTOGRAPHER OF THE YEAR 2012

Mateus Piesiak Poland
Special mention

Above. My family and I go to the Austrian Alps every year for our winter holiday. One night I went to photograph the night landscape. The clear air showed millions of stars in the sky.

Right. One evening, walking in the forest at sunset, I caught a glimpse of a long-eared owl, which sat on the beautifully lighted branch. I always carry my camera with me, so I didn't miss the opportunity!

Austrian Alps. **Mateusz Piesiak, Poland (age 16).**
Canon 90D with 400mm lens; f5.6; 1/125s; ISO 640.

Abu Dhabi, United Arab Emirates. **Nasser Albahrani, Abu Dhabi (age 18).**
Canon 5D Mark II with 24-70mm lens; f14; 1/50s; ISO 160.

YOUNG TRAVEL PHOTOGRAPHER OF THE YEAR 2012

Nasser Albahrani Abu Dhabi
Special mention

Left. Reading the holy Quran in the Sheikh Zayed Grand Mosque, just as dawn starts to illuminate the place.

Below. Someone praying to God in the Sheikh Zayed Grand Mosque, just a few minutes before sunrise.

Abu Dhabi, United Arab Emirates. **Nasser Albahrani, Abu Dhabi (age 18).** *Canon 450D with 10-20mm lens; f16; 1/6s; ISO 400.*

Peach Bottom, Pennsylvania, USA. **Chase Guttman, USA (age 16).**
Nikon D7000 with 80-200mm lens; f6.3; 1/640s; ISO 1250.

Peach Bottom, Pennsylvania, USA. **Chase Guttman, USA (age 16).**
Nikon D7000 with 80-200mm lens; f5; 1/400s; ISO 320.

Peach Bottom, Pennsylvania, USA. **Chase Guttman, USA (age 16).**
Nikon D7000 with 80-200mm lens; f9; 1/320s; ISO 800.

Peach Bottom, Pennsylvania, USA. **Chase Guttman, USA (age 16)**. *Nikon D7000 with 80-200mm lens; f6.3; 1/640s; ISO 1250.*

YOUNG TRAVEL PHOTOGRAPHER OF THE YEAR 2012

Chase Guttman USA
Emerging Talent Award

This page. Ruddy cheeks provide the few vibrant hues to be found amongst the Plain People's sombre black garb at a crowded assembly of auction attendees.

Opposite page, top left. An elder stoops for eye contact as distant generations exchange wisdom and discuss farm equipment to be auctioned at an Amish mud sale – a springtime ritual held before the season's first ploughing.

Opposite page, top right. At a premier equine event in Lancaster County, thrusting limbs and flying manes grab the attention of all ages.

Opposite page, bottom. Among a sea of straw hats, soulful Amish eyes take a break from the action in the pen, where farm mules are put through their paces in hopes of a high bid.

PEOPLE WATCHING
PORTFOLIO 2012

The simplicity, serenity and beauty of Philip Lee Harvey's images is striking. Composition, combined with clever use of depth of field, complement the warm, soft light giving the images a remarkable quality and sense of occasion as the villagers work together to bring in the groundnut harvest.

Sponsors of this award:

Adobe, Digimarc, Plastic Sandwich

Near Bagan, Burma. **Philip Lee Harvey, UK.** *Canon EOS 5D Mark II with 70-200mm lens; f5; 1/125s; ISO 160.*

Near Bagan, Burma. **Philip Lee Harvey, UK.** *Canon EOS 5D Mark II with 70-200mm lens; f7.1; 1/320s; ISO 160.*

PEOPLE WATCHING
PORTFOLIO 2012

Philip Lee Harvey UK
Winner

Page 25. In November, the community gathers together to harvest groundnuts. The process hasn't changed for generations and everyone helps to harvest each other's fields. First, the farmer ploughs the field with bullocks to pull up the groundnut roots, then workers pick up the loose roots by hand.

Opposite page. After the roots have been dug up they are placed on a lattice table.

Below. The farmers beat the groundnut roots, allowing the nuts to fall through the lattice table into baskets placed beneath.

Right. Finally, the farmer stands atop a large wooden tripod and sifts the heavy nuts from the lighter earth, which blows away. Groundnuts are harvested for roasting and eating, but also to produce nut oils.

Near Bagan, Burma. **Philip Lee Harvey, UK.** *Canon EOS 5D Mark II with 70-200mm lens; f5; 1/250s; ISO 320.*

Near Bagan, Burma. **Philip Lee Harvey, UK.** *Canon EOS 5D Mark II with 70-200mm lens; f4.5; 1/640s; ISO 160.*

Omo River Valley, Ethiopia. **Jan Schlegel, Germany.** *Ebony field SV45T1 4x5 inch camera with Schneider Super Symmar 150mm XL lens; f22; 1/30s; ISO 400.*

Omo River Valley, Ethiopia. **Jan Schlegel, Germany.** *Ebony field SV45T1 4x5 inch camera with Schneider Super Symmar 150mm XL lens; f16; 1/30s; ISO 400.*

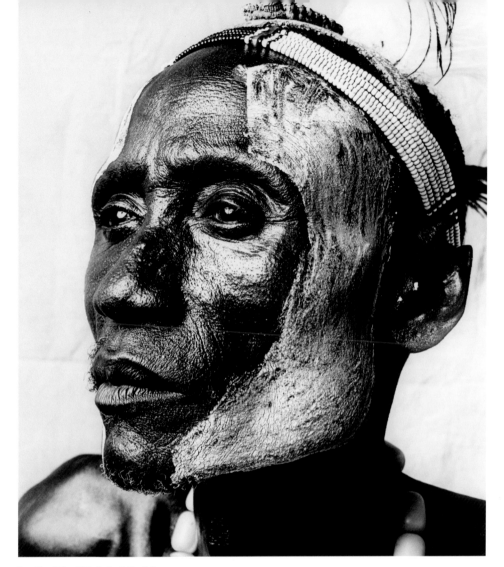

Omo River Valley, Ethiopia. **Jan Schlegel, Germany.**
Ebony field SV45T1 4x5 inch camera with Schneider Super Symmar 150mm XL lens; f22; 1/30s; ISO 400.

Omo River Valley, Ethiopia. **Jan Schlegel, Germany.** *Ebony field SV45T1 4x5 inch camera with Schneider Super Symmar 150mm XL lens; f22; 1/30s; ISO 400.*

PEOPLE WATCHING
PORTFOLIO 2012

Jan Schlegel Germany
Runner Up

In these black-and-white silverprints of the Karo tribe, none of the subjects wore special make-up or were specially dressed before the photos were taken. Nothing was staged, nothing is fake. The image compositions – the highly-contrasted play of light and shadow, the inner dynamics and the extraordinary perspectives – open a crack in the door of the secret treasures of this world that are becoming increasingly difficult to find.

West Papua New Guinea. **Anders Ryman, Sweden.** *Canon 1VS with 17-35mm lens; ISO 1000.*

West Papua New Guinea. **Anders Ryman, Sweden.** *Canon 1VS with 17-35mm lens; ISO 1000.*

PEOPLE WATCHING
PORTFOLIO 2012

Anders Ryman Sweden
Highly Commended

Above. Two Kombai men collect sago grubs which are a delicacy.

Left. A Kombai man holds up a lizard pierced by the arrow that shot it down.

Western Wall of Jerusalem, Israel. **Jordi Cohen, Spain.** *Canon EOS 5D Mark II with 16-35mm lens; f6.3; 1/500s; ISO 1250.*

Old City of Jerusalem, Israel. **Jordi Cohen, Spain.** *Canon EOS 5D Mark II with 16-35mm lens; f2.8; 1/40s; ISO 2000.*

PEOPLE WATCHING PORTFOLIO 2012

Jordi Cohen Spain
Commended

Above. Amshinover Rebbe and his followers at the Western Wall in the Old City of Jerusalem.

Left. Hasidic Jews talking in front of the Old City walls of Jerusalem, near the Jaffa Gate.

WILD PLANET
PORTFOLIO 2012

Wow! In the absence of any ambient light pollution every detail of the heavens can be seen. Marsel van Oosten's portfolio is skillfully crafted, as the photographer introduces just enough controlled lighting to bring the natural world to life with majestic beauty.

Sponsors of this award:

Explore, Adobe, Digimarc, Plastic Sandwich

Namib desert, Namibia. **Marsel van Oosten, Netherlands.** *Nikon D3S with 14-24mm lens; f2.8; 30s; ISO 3200.*

Namib desert, Namibia. **Marsel van Oosten, Netherlands.** *Nikon D3S with 14-24mm lens; f2.8; 30s; ISO 3200.*

WILD PLANET
PORTFOLIO 2012

Marsel Van Oosten Netherlands
Winner

The quiver tree is a species of aloe indigenous to Namibia that occurs in parts of the Namib desert around the South African-Namibian border. These images were shot at night with the use of some small flashlights. Namibia is perfect for night photography because of the dry desert air and the lack of light pollution.

Namib desert, Namibia. **Marsel van Oosten, Netherlands.** *Nikon D3S with 14-24mm lens; f2.8; 30s; ISO 3200.*

Namib desert, Namibia. **Marsel van Oosten, Netherlands.** *Nikon D3S with 14-24mm lens; f2.8; 30s; ISO 3200.*

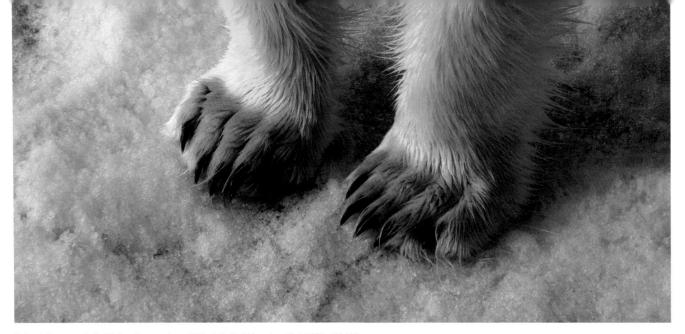

Svalbard, Norwegian Arctic. **Uli Kunz, Germany.** *Canon 5D Mark II with 300mm lens; f9; 1/1600s; ISO 200.*

Svalbard, Norwegian Arctic. **Uli Kunz, Germany.** *Canon 5D Mark II with 17-40mm lens; f22; 1/50s; ISO 160.*

WILD PLANET
PORTFOLIO 2012

Uli Kunz Germany
Runner Up

Opposite page, top. My aim was to photograph only parts of the animal – to highlight the subtle details of this Queen of the Arctic.

Opposite page, bottom. Polar bears may look cuddly, but their formidable teeth show their true nature – the carcass of this young bear, which had starved to death, was found on the beach.

Top right. On this foggy, overcast day the light was very soft, which allowed me to capture the bear's reflection in the water when she slowly leaned down and sniffed at the ice edge.

Bottom right. This polar bear mother approached our boat in the pack ice off Svalbard. She had two gorgeous one year-old cubs with her, who were equally as inquisitive.

Svalbard, Norwegian Arctic. **Uli Kunz, Germany.** *Canon 5D Mark II with 300mm lens; f9; 1/100s; ISO 200.*

Svalbard, Norwegian Arctic. **Uli Kunz, Germany.** *Canon 5D Mark II with 300mm lens; f9; 1/2000s; ISO 200.*

Kribi, Cameroon. **Arne Strømme, Norway.** *Nikon D200 with 80-200mm lens; f10; 1/15s; ISO 400.*

Kribi, Cameroon. **Arne Strømme, Norway.**
Nikon D200 with 80-200mm lens; f13; 1/15s; ISO 400.

WILD PLANET
PORTFOLIO 2012

Arne Strømme Norway
Highly Commended

Red Kite hunting for fish in the harbour of this small fishing village. I tried to capture the atmosphere rather than take documentary images. It's not the first time I've taken this style of picture – in fact, it's actually more the rule than the exception, and is definitely the way I like to shoot.

Spitsbergen, Norway. **Michal Jastrzebski, Poland.** *Nikon D3S with VR600mm lens; f8; 1/1250s; ISO 1000.*

Spitsbergen, Norway. **Michal Jastrzebski, Poland.** *Nikon D3S with VR600mm lens; f7.1; 1/1600s; ISO 2000.*

WILD PLANET
PORTFOLIO 2012

Michal Jastrzebski Poland
Commended

Above. Purple sandpiper resting.

Left. Arctic fox scavenging on a ringed-seal
carcass left by a polar bear.

JOURNEYS PORTFOLIO 2012

Journeys was our first open portfolio category in the awards, and photographers were invited to submit their own personal collection of travel photographs. The entries were diverse, with Lung Liu's Burning Man portfolio catching the eye for its other-worldly images full of gentle elegance and minimalism.

Sponsors of this award:

Fujifilm, Adobe, Digimarc, Plastic Sandwich

Black Rock City, Nevada, USA. **Lung Liu, Canada.** *Pentax K20D with 28mm lens; f2.8; 1.8s; ISO 800.*

Black Rock City, Nevada, USA. **Lung Liu, Canada.** *Pentax K20D with 29mm lens; f8; 1/500s; ISO 200.*

JOURNEYS PORTFOLIO 2012

Lung Liu Canada
Winner

Page 41. Black Rock City becomes Nevada's third-largest city for one week every year during the Burning Man festival. This event now draws in a following that borders on the religious.

Left. View from the altar of the Temple of Juno. The temple is built for attendees to place letters, photos and other mementos to loved ones that have passed away, and will be burned on the final day of the festivities.

Top right. A midday view of the desert. Prominent art installations include the Temple of Juno and the Wall Street Project.

Bottom right. A blue moon rises over an art installation far away from the festivities. The artist of the installation was married here later that week.

Black Rock City, Nevada, USA. **Lung Liu, Canada.** *Pentax K20D with 50mm lens; f10; 1/1500s; ISO 200.*

Black Rock City, Nevada, USA. **Lung Liu, Canada.** *Pentax K20D with 28mm lens; f2.8; 1.8s; ISO 800.*

Iquitos, Loreto Region, Maynas Province, Northern Peru. **Jason Edwards, Australia.** *Pentax K-7k with 10-20mm lens; f7.1; 1/10s; ISO 160.*

Iquitos, Loreto Region, Maynas Province, Northern Peru. **Jason Edwards, Australia.** *Pentax K-7k with 10-20mm lens; f6.3; 0.5s; ISO 320.*

Iquitos, Loreto Region, Maynas Province, Northern Peru. **Jason Edwards, Australia.** *Pentax K-7k with 10-20mm lens; f7.1; 1/8s; ISO 100.*

JOURNEYS PORTFOLIO 2012

Jason Edwards Australia
Runner Up

Top left. A terrified pygmy marmoset for sale in an Amazonian river market where speakers belt out hip-hop music.

Top right. What is a life worth? This jaguar skin was sold for US $25 In Peru.

Left. A pharmacopeia selling everything from snakes to turtles.

Opposite page. Amazonian parrots sweltering in a plastic tub for sale at 25 cents each.

Iquitos, Loreto Region, Maynas Province, Northern Peru. **Jason Edwards, Australia.** *Pentax K-7k with 10-20mm lens; f7.1; 1/10s; ISO 160.*

Balkan Mountain range, Bulgaria. **Timothy Allen, UK.** *Canon 5D Mark II with 16mm lens; f7.1; 1/1000s; ISO 320.*

JOURNEYS
PORTFOLIO 2012

Timothy Allen UK
Highly Commended

Buzludzha (pronounced Buz'ol'ja) is Bulgaria's largest ideological monument to Communism. It took 6,000 workers seven years to build it. In 1989, Bulgaria's bloodless revolution ended with the disbandment of the Bulgarian Communist Party. Ownership of the monument was ceded to the state and consequently it was left to ruin. Today, this incredible derelict building stands as an iconic monument to an abandoned ideology.

Balkan Mountain range, Bulgaria. **Timothy Allen, UK.** *Canon 5D Mark II with 16mm lens; f6.3; 1/5000s; ISO 640.*

JOURNEYS
PORTFOLIO 2012

Tom McLaughlan UK
Commended

Below. Columns at a bar in Bologna's Porta Europa, rotated through 90 degrees.

Below right. The Maxxi Museum in Rome is Italy's national museum of the 21st century arts.

Bologna, Italy. **Tom McLaughlan, UK.** *Canon 5D Mark II with 70-200mm lens; f13; 0.4s; ISO 250.*

Rome, Italy. **Tom McLaughlan, UK.** *Canon 5D Mark II with 70-200mm lens; f7.1; 1/40s; ISO 200.*

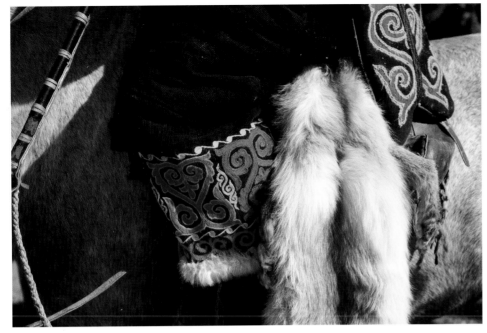

Near Sagsai, Ulgii, Bayan-Ulgii, Mongolia. **Rupert Sagar-Musgrave, UK.** *Canon 5D Mark I with 24-105mm lens; f5; 1/400s; ISO 100.*

Jerez, Andalucia, Spain. **Rupert Sagar-Musgrave, UK.** *Canon 50D with 70-200mm lens; f5.6; 1/800s; ISO 100.*

JOURNEYS PORTFOLIO 2012

Rupert Sagar-Musgrave UK
Commended

Above left. Kazakh eagle hunters, from western Mongolia, train their golden eagles to hunt for small prey such as rabbits, foxes and young wolves.

Left. Detail of a smartly dressed couple on horseback at the annual Jerez Horse Fair.

ONE SHOT 2012
WATER

Water is an evocative theme which can be interpreted in many ways, as the selection of winning images demonstrates. Hilde Foss's image was chosen as the winner; the energy and sense of movement is palpable while the image remains delightfully abstract.

Sponsors of this award:

Fujifilm, Adobe

Voss, Norway. **Hilde Foss, Norway.** *Canon 7D with 70-300mm lens; f5.6; 1/8000s; ISO 640.*

Djenne, Mali. **Timothy Allen, UK.** *Canon EOS 5D Mark II with 16-35mm lens; f6.3; 1/320s; ISO 640.*

ONE SHOT 2012
WATER

Hilde Foss Norway
Winner

Previous page
A kayaker enters the Brandseth River for the downhill competition at the Voss Extreme Sports Week in Norway. The competitors enter via a ramp in an otherwise calm part of the river, creating this great wall of clear water.

ONE SHOT 2012
WATER

Timothy Allen UK
Runner Up

A man waters his garden in the desert outside Djenne in the dry season.

Jökulsárlón, glacial lagoon, Iceland. **Joshua Holko, Australia.** *Canon EOS 1DS Mark III with 24mm lens; f11; 1.3s; ISO 100.*

ONE SHOT 2012
WATER

Joshua Holko Australia
Highly Commended

A large iceberg that has carved off the Vatnajokull glacier
and washed ashore on the black volcanic beach near the
Jökulsárlón glacial lagoon. Backlit by the sun and glowing
from within, the iceberg is reflected in the sand as a storm
rolls in from the ocean.

Galle, Sri Lanka. **Kimberley Coole, UK.** *Canon 5D Mark II with 24-105mm lens; f4; 11.5s; ISO 160.*

ONE SHOT - WATER

Kimberley Coole UK
Commended

Stilt fishing is a traditional practice found mainly in the Galle area of Sri Lanka. As my time passed in Sri Lanka, the weather only worsened. Time was rapidly running out, so I made the decision to use the stormy skies and rough seas to my advantage. The long exposure gives the image more atmosphere and mystery.

ONE SHOT - WATER

Timothy Allen UK
Commended

Samnieng, a Laos fisherman, crosses the turbulent Mekong River to reach his fishing grounds. During the rainy season the river swells horrendously, rendering many of the prime fishing spots dangerously inaccessible, but for the efforts of the few brave and/or foolish fishermen who dare to venture where the majority fear to go.

Four Thousand Islands, Laos. **Timothy Allen, UK.** *Canon EOS 5D Mark II with 400mm lens; f5.7; 1/8000s; ISO 640.*

NEW TALENT 2012
ANOTHER WORLD

The New Talent category encourages and supports photographers who aspire to make the step from amateur or semi-professional to a career in photography. The photo-journalist skill of storytelling through pictures is a key tool for any professional photographer and the judges look for this quality within the portfolios. Alessandra Meniconzi's collection captures life for Siberia's Nenet community in images that tell a story, but also include eye-catching angles ideal for headlining an article.

Sponsors of this award:

Tribes Travel, Fujifilm, Adobe, Digimarc, Plastic Sandwich, Photo Iconic, Young Photographers' Alliance

*Siberia, Russia. **Alessandra Meniconzi, Switzerland.** Canon EOS 1DS Mark III with 24-70mm lens; f8; 1/800s; ISO 100.*

Siberia, Russia. **Alessandra Meniconzi, Switzerland.** *Canon EOS 1DS Mark III with 16-35mm lens; f8; 1/200s; ISO 100.*

NEW TALENT 2012
ANOTHER WORLD

Alessandra Meniconzi Switzerland
Winner

Previous page
The Nenets use reindeer for almost all of their everyday needs, from food and clothing to tools and transportation. Herds are about 70–100 strong.

Siberia, Russia. **Alessandra Meniconzi, Switzerland.**
Canon EOS 1DS Mark III with 24-70mm lens; f/5.0; 1/10 sec; ISO 400

Siberia, Russia. **Alessandra Meniconzi, Switzerland.**
Canon EOS 1DS Mark III with 24-70mm lens; f5; 1/10s; ISO 400.

Siberia, Russia. **Alessandra Meniconzi, Switzerland.**
Canon EOS 1DS Mark III with 24-70mm lens; f5; 1/100s; ISO 100.

Opposite page. Every member of the family is assigned their own chores: this young Nenet girl is collecting wood.

Top left. The Nenets live in 'chums', temporary conical dwellings made from reindeer skin and fur, supported by a long wooden post.

Middle left. Sveta talks about an imaginary line called a 'sangi', that runs through the tent and which women cannot cross because bad luck will fall on the chum (tent) and the family that live within it.

Bottom left. Raw reindeer meat is considered a true delight and an old Nenet proverb says if you don't eat the fresh meat and hot blood of reindeer, you'll be condemned to die in the tundra.

Below. Skins of slaughtered reindeer are sold to the tanneries in Salekhard and some of the meat to butchers in Moscow.

Siberia, Russia. **Alessandra Meniconzi, Switzerland.**
Canon EOS 1DS Mark III with 24-70mm lens; f7.1; 1/200s; ISO 100.

Patan, Nepal. **Giorgio Bianchi, Italy.** *Nikon D700 with 24-70mm lens; f13; 1/200s; ISO 400.*

NEW TALENT 2012
ANOTHER WORLD

Giorgio Bianchi Italy
Runner Up

Above. I spent three days living with the people who scour this rubbish dump, on the outskirts of Kathmandu and Patan, for plastic, metal and glass that they can sell on for a few rupees.

Right. I spied this group of women weaving carpets on a loom while I was wandering through the little lanes of Patan.

Patan, Nepal. **Giorgio Bianchi, Italy.** *Nikon D700; 24-70mm lens; f2.8; 1/100s; ISO 1600.*

Kathmandu, Nepal. **Giorgio Bianchi, Italy.** *Nikon D700 with 24-70mm lens; f4; 1/250s; ISO 400.*

Bhaktapur, Nepal. **Giorgio Bianchi, Italy.** *Nikon D700 with 24-70mm lens; f16; 1/250s; ISO 400.*

Above. Early morning craftsmen and sellers at Kathmandu market.

Left. In a corner of the famous Pottery Square in Bhaktapur, a group of relatives enjoy a well-deserved rest after an intense day of pottery making.

Route One, Iceland. **Catherine Sales, UK.**
Mamiya 645 1000S with 45mm lens; f9; 1/1250s; ISO 400.

Route One, Iceland. **Catherine Sales, UK.**
Mamiya 645 1000S with 45mm lens; f8; 1/320s; ISO 400.

Route One, Iceland. **Catherine Sales, UK.** *Mamiya 645 1000S with 45mm lens; f8; 1/800s; ISO 400.*

NEW TALENT 2012
ANOTHER WORLD

Catherine Sales UK
Highly Commended

Route One is an 830-mile road surrounding Iceland. At times I felt I was the only one on this never-ending, desolate stretch of road and I felt inspired to record such a landscape. I became drawn to objects I wouldn't look twice at in ordinary circumstances, such as telephone poles, fire hydrants, and bus stops. These and the ever-changing landscape became my inspiration and my focus throughout my journey.

Cocos Island, Costa-Rica. **Dmitry Miroshnikov, Russia.** *Canon 5D Mark II with 16-35mm lens; f20; 1/200s; ISO 800.*

NEW TALENT 2012
ANOTHER WORLD

Dmitry Miroshnikov Russia
Commended

Above. Curious boobies looking down on what is happening below – dolphins are on a hunt.

Far left. The sardines attempt to get away from the predators by swimming up to the surface but are picked off by gannets divebombing into the water.

Left. Dolphins herding the sardines into a 'bait ball', which they then swim through with their mouths open to gulp up their prey.

Port St. Johns, South Africa. **Dmitry Miroshnikov, Russia.**
Canon 5D Mark II with 16-35mm lens; f6.3; 1/200s; ISO 800.

Port St. Johns, South Africa. **Dmitry Miroshnikov, Russia.**
Canon 5D Mark II with 16-35mm lens; f8; 1/200s; ISO 400.

CONDÉ NAST TRAVELLER AWARD - CELEBRATION

This special award was created to mark Condé Nast Traveller magazine's 15th anniversary, with the theme 'Celebration'. Enrique Lopez Tapia's portfolio of images draws you right into the heart of the action, capturing the power and speed of Galicia's Rapa das Bestas - a centuries-old celebration of the bond between man and horse.

Sponsors of this award:

Condé Nast Traveller

Sabucedo, Galicia, Spain. **Enrique López-Tapia, Spain.** Nikon D300 with 18-135mm lens; f36; 1/3s; ISO 200.

Sabucedo, Galicia, Spain. **Enrique López-Tapia, Spain.** *Nikon D300 with 18-135mm lens; f5.6; 1/30s; ISO 400.*

CONDÉ NAST TRAVELLER
AWARD - CELEBRATION

Enrique Lopez Tapia Spain
Winner

Previous page. The Rapa das Bestas is a centuries-old celebration from the region of Galicia, in northern Spain. Every July, wild horses are rounded up so their tail and mane hair can be cut. The animals are not restrained with reins or bridles – just the strength and ingenuity of man.

Sabucedo, Galicia, Spain. **Enrique López-Tapia, Spain.**
Nikon D300 with 70-200mm lens; f2.8; 1/250s; ISO 200.

Sabucedo, Galicia, Spain. **Enrique López-Tapia, Spain.**
Nikon D300 with 12-24mm lens; f4; 1/320s; ISO 200.

Sabucedo, Galicia, Spain. **Enrique López-Tapia, Spain.**
Nikon D300 with 70-200mm lens; f2.8; 1/500s; ISO 200.

Sabucedo, Galicia, Spain. **Enrique López-Tapia, Spain.**
Nikon D300 with 18-135mm lens; f5.6; 1/200s; ISO 200.

Opposite page. Hundreds of horses run through the streets of Sabucedo towards the corral where the cutting occurs.

Top left. The men caress and whisper to the horses to reassure them while their manes are being cut.

Above left. The horses are locked in a large pen together, as men – known as *aloitadores* – choose the best specimens.

Top right. The horses become very territorial when confined in the pens and confrontations between the males are very common.

Above right. Aloitadores wrestling with the horses.

Bete Giyorgis, Lalibela, Ethiopia. **Alessandra Meniconzi, Switzerland.** *Canon EOS 1DS Mark III with 24-70mm lens; f8; 10s; ISO 200.*

Lalibela, Ethiopia. **Alessandra Meniconzi, Switzerland.** *Canon EOS 1DS Mark III with 16-35mm lens; f5; 1/12s; ISO 100.*

Lalibela, Ethiopia. **Alessandra Meniconzi, Switzerland.** *Canon EOS 1DS Mark III with 24-70mm lens; f5.6; 1/40s; ISO 100.*

CONDÉ NAST TRAVELLER AWARD - CELEBRATION

Alessandra Meniconzi Switzerland
Runner Up

Opposite page. Lalibela is one of Ethiopia's holiest cities and famous for its 11 UNESCO-listed medieval monolithic churches carved out of rock. One of the most impressive is the Church of St George.

Top left. The churches are carved, inside and out, from soft volcanic rock and connected to each other by small passages and tunnels.

Top right. Priests showing the carved cross inside Bete Maryam (House Of Mary), built in 1166.

Bottom left. Lalibela is a magnet for Ethiopian Christian pilgrims.

Lalibela, Ethiopia. **Alessandra Meniconzi, Switzerland.** *Canon EOS 1DS Mark III with 24-70mm lens; f4; 1/32s; ISO 100.*

Burning Man Festival, Black Rock City, Nevada, USA. **Lung Liu, Canada.**
Pentax K20D with 28mm lens; f4; 1.45s; ISO 800.

Burning Man Festival, Black Rock City, Nevada, USA. **Lung Liu, Canada.**
Pentax K20D with 29mm lens; f8; 1.8s; ISO 1600.

Burning Man Festival, Black Rock City, Nevada, USA. **Lung Liu, Canada.**
Pentax K20D with 29mm lens; f8; 1/1000s; ISO 1600.

CONDÉ NAST TRAVELLER AWARD - CELEBRATION

Lung Liu Canada
Highly Commended

Opposite page. Kathryn June dancing in a feathered costume inside the Temple of Juno. Kathryn embraces mourners within her wings at the temple's final sunrise before it is put to flames later that night.

Top. Shayla Hayashi is a veteran burner with whom I shared the same theme camp. I took this portrait of her as we explored the desert after sunset.

Middle. To a large number of veteran burners, the Temple of Juno is the emotional and spiritual epicenter of the festival and performances like these are tinged with something bordering on the sacred.

Bottom. Strange and elaborate weddings are extremely common at Burning Man.

Burning Man Festival, Black Rock City, Nevada, USA. **Lung Liu, Canada.** *Pentax K20D with 22mm lens; f4.5; 1/90s; ISO 200.*

FIRST SHOT 2012
BIG CITY

The First Shot category is for less-experienced amateur photographers who are still learning their craft. The judges choose a winner on the basis that their image shows great potential. Anka Sliwa's image is wonderfully observed and captures a moment which every viewer can identify with, in an environment where we are increasingly engrossed in mobile technology.

Sponsors of this award:

Fujifilm, Adobe, Photo Iconic

Shoreditch, London, England. **Anka Sliwa, UK.** *Nikon D80 with 17-50mm lens; f2.8; 1/160s ISO 400.*

Brick Lane, London, England. **Nadia Townshend, UK.** *Canon EOS 1000D with 18-55mm lens; f16; 1/160s; ISO 200.*

FIRST SHOT 2012
BIG CITY

Previous page
Anka Sliwa UK
Winner

Previous Page. Man walking past Ben Slow's 'Screaming Faces' painting on a wall in Hanbury Street. This graffiti itself composes a very powerful image. One can almost hear screams coming out of the two mouths. I needed a figure that would make the silent scream audible. This casual passer-by seemed perfect.

FIRST SHOT 2012
BIG CITY

Nadia Townshend UK
Runner Up

Above. I was out exploring the alleyways behind Brick Lane when I stumbled upon this woman sitting atop a chimney. I was concerned as to why she should be sitting on such a dangerous perch, but in a fleeting moment I managed to get a shot.

FIRST SHOT 2012
BIG CITY

Natasha Semmence UK
Runner up

This page. Rush hour inside Waterloo underground station. Everyone is hurrying home, heads down and anonymous. It's a frenzy of activity, yet no one stops. As one person leaves the steps, another replaces them. It's a constant conveyor belt of people and movement.

Southbank, London, England. **Natasha Semmence, UK.** *Canon 450D with 18-55mm lens; f5.6; 1.6s; ISO 800.*

London, England. **Monica Chien, Taiwan.** *Apple iPhone 4S; f2; 1/15s; ISO 800.*

FIRST SHOT 2012
BIG CITY

Monica Chien Taiwan
Commended

Standing atop the balcony of a theatre in London's West End, I couldn't help but notice the beautiful vista below. The panorama is symbolic of this great city – a city of contrast, diversity, and architectural variance spanning centuries.

Victoria Harbour, Hong Kong. **Agne Subelyte, Switzerland.** *Fujifilm Finepix F10 with 36mm lens; f5.6; 1/680s; ISO 80.*

FIRST SHOT 2012
BIG CITY

Agne Subelyte Switzerland
Commended

It was January 2012 and I had just arrived in Hong Kong for a 6-month business trip. Right away I hit the crowded streets of this amazing city. I enjoyed observing the people and their diversity, their everlasting flow, and the way all that noise and movement seemed to dissolve in the eternity of a hazy sunset.

BEST SINGLE IMAGE
IN A PORTFOLIO 2012

Each year there are many portfolio entries which don't win prizes, but which contain outstanding individual images. In 2012, these images were chosen from the three portfolio categories along with others which merit a special mention.

Sponsors of this award:

Adobe, Genesis Imaging, Royal Geographical Society (with IBG)

Masai Mara, Kenya. **David Lazar, Australia.** *Nikon D700m with 24-84mm lens; f7.1; 1/200s; ISO 400.*

JOURNEYS

David Lazar Australia
Special Mention

Previous page. Three Masai boys help each other climb to the top of a boulder overlooking the plains of the Masai Mara. I prefer to imagine the photo first and then set it up accordingly.

PEOPLE WATCHING

Timothy Allen UK
Best Single Image

I was making a film for Oxfam in Grand Jedeh province interviewing a lady in her village when hundreds of children came to watch. I shot the picture while they were all jostling for a viewpoint.

Grand Gedeh, Liberia. **Timothy Allen, UK.** *Canon 5D Mark II with 85mm lens; f5.6; 1/250s; ISO 640.*

PEOPLE WATCHING

Timothy Allen UK
Special Mention

This young girl is sipping *airag* - fermented mare's milk drunk every day by Mongolians.

PEOPLE WATCHING

Jino Lee Malaysia
Special Mention

Salt farmers from Kusamba, Bali. Most keep roosters as pets and occasionally they will bring them out for a friendly sparring session after a hard day's work. The chickens don't wear blades on their feet, so none of the birds are harmed.

Bali, Indonesia. **Jino Lee, Malaysia.** *Canon EOS1DX with 24-70mm lens; f7.1; 1/250s; ISO 640.*

Blue River Valley, Mongolia. **Timothy Allen, UK.**
Canon EOS 5D Mark II with 85mm lens; f11; 1/320s; ISO 640.

Iquitos, Maynas Province, Northern Peru. **Jason Edwards, Australia.**
Pentax K-7k with 10-20mm lens; f7.1; 1/10s; ISO 160.

JOURNEYS

Jason Edwards Australia
Special Mention

Amazonian rainforest parrots sweltering in a plastic tub where they are for sale for 25 cents each. Of the birds that survive many find themselves in the illegal pet trades of Europe and the USA.

Udaipur, Rajasthan, India. **Carlos Esteves, Portugal.**
Canon EOS 40D with 17-85mm lens; f5.6; 1/250s; ISO 400.

JOURNEYS

Carlos Esteves Portugal
Special Mention

I was wandering around a small fruit and vegetable market in Udaipur, when I was attracted to the hands of this old woman holding a purple onion the exact same tone as her dress.

Dhaka, Bangladesh. **Jonathan Munshi, USA.**
Nikon D300 with 16-85mm lens; f10; 1/60s; ISO 800.

JOURNEYS

Jonathan Munshi USA
Special Mention

During the tenuous lull between waves of monsoon rain, busy life returns briefly to the streets of Dhaka.

Siberut Island, West Sumatra, Indonesia. **Andrew Newey, UK.** *Canon EOS 5D Mark II with 50mm lens; f18; 1/2700s; ISO 320.*

JOURNEYS

Andrew Newey UK
Best Single Image

Siberut, the largest of the Mentawai Islands in West Sumatra, is home to the vanishing Mentawai people. They live a semi-nomadic hunter-gatherer lifestyle deep in the rainforest and practice a form of animism known as Jarayak. It took us three days of hard trekking to reach the village.

Spitsbergen, Norway. **Michal Jastrzebski, Poland.** *Nikon D3S with VR600mm lens; f9; 1/1250s; ISO 1600.*

WILD PLANET

Michal Jastrzebski Poland
Best Single Image

Opposite page. When the polar bear finished eating, Arctic foxes came and began scavenging on the seal remains. Smaller individuals then arrived, followed by these gulls.

WILD PLANET

Daisy Gilardini Switzerland
Special Mention

Top right. Every year in October/November in Wapusk National Park, hundreds of polar bears gather around Hudson Bay and wait for the water to freeze so they can hunt seals. Usually solitary animals, during this period their interactions are frequent, and young males can often be observed sparring. In my images I try to achieve simplicity, and by overexposing the image I isolate the subject and create a strong tension in the subject's lines and shapes.

WILD PLANET

Theo Bosboom Netherlands
Special Mention

Bottom right. A fulmar flying above a black lava beach in a blizzard in winter. I was very much attracted by the graphic lines of the snow, the black sand and the water. The fulmar completed the picture, showing that, even in a harsh environment like this, birds can survive.

Wapusk National Park, Manitoba, Canada. **Daisy Gilardini, Switzerland.** *Nikon D3 with 200-400mm lens; f6.3; 1/1000s; ISO 2000.*

Between Höfn and Djupivogur, Iceland. **Theo Bosboom, Netherlands.** *Canon 1D Mark IV with 70-200mm lens; f6.3; 1/1250s; ISO 2000.*

Kiskunsagi National Park, Hungary. **Sue Flood, UK.** *Canon 1DS3 with 600mm lens; f8; 1/13s; ISO 125.*

Mashatu Game Reserve, Botswana. **Chris McLennan, New Zealand.** *Canon EOS 1DX with 300mm lens; f4; 1/4000s; ISO 800.*

WILD PLANET

Sue Flood UK
Special Mention

Left. I was photographing birds in Hungary, and was up very early one morning to go and watch the herons. I had taken lots (and lots!) of fast-shutter speed shots of the heron fishing, but suddenly realised that the images which froze the action didn't really capture the spirit of this lovely bird. I experimented with slower shutter speeds and this shot was the result.

WILD PLANET

Sebastian Beun Belgium
Special Mention

Opposite page. The Great Grey Owl, also known as the 'Phantom of the North', gazes intensely at the camera.

WILD PLANET

Chris McLennan New Zealand
Special Mention

Left. Three large cheetah cubs run gracefully as their mother looks on. The back lighting and dust combined with the speed of the animals made this a difficult shot to achieve, but also makes it more special.

Pairi Daiza Wildlife Reserve, Burgelette, Hainaut, Belgium. **Sebastian Beun, Belgium.** *Canon EOS 5D Mark II with 100-400mm lens; f5.6; 1/125s; ISO 320.*

JUDGES

The TPOTY judging panel is international and made up of experts from the world of photography and travel. They are selected to reflect a variety of backgrounds, styles and attitudes to photography and the photographic image. A key element of the panel is the wealth of visual and specialist expertise brought into the mix by our technical and creative judges. Lay judges and past winners have also participated, bringing fresh views and perspectives to the judging process.

These judges give their time because they are passionate about photography, and we are immensely grateful for their efforts.

We would like to thank the 2012 judging panel:

Judges

Steve Bloom - travel & wildlife photographer

Chris Coe - photographer, author & lecturer

Colin Finlay - head of World Illustrated at photoshot.com

Jeremy Hoare - photographer & TV camerman

Jason Hawkes - award-winning aerial photographer

Debbie Ireland - picture editor & curator

Eamonn McCabe - award-winning photographer & picture editor

Nick Meers - landscape & panoramic photographer

Caroline Metcalfe - director of photography, Condé Nast Traveller

Mary Robert - head of photography, American International University

Jerry Tavin - founder, Young Photographers' Alliance & Glasshouse Images

Emma Thomson - award-winning travel writer & editor

Ami Vitale - award-winning photojournalist

Steve Watkins - photographer & editor, Outdoor Photography

Chris Weston - wildlife photographer

Manfred Zollner - managing editor, Fotomagazin

Left. The North Pole. **Nick Smith, UK.**

SPONSORS AND PARTNERS

Cutty Sark

Cutty Sark blended Scotch is an iconic whisky; its distinctive yellow label has graced the world's best bars and clubs for nearly 90 years. The first light-coloured blended whisky, it was launched at the height of cocktail culture in the 1920s and it has remained synonymous with enjoying great drinks in great company ever since. The brand keeps cropping up in popular culture, a constant reminder of the status of the brand. It is always the choice of adventurous characters! Cutty Sark's major markets are now Spain, Greece, Portugal, and the USA.

www.cutty-sark.com

Yosemite/Mariposa Co. Tourism Bureau

Just three hours from San Francisco, Yosemite National Park beholds four seasons of splendor. Take in the wonders of one of America's greatest national treasures with a guided naturalist hike, photography class, snowshoe trek or a high country walk. Enhance your visit with a mountain bike ride, a walk in the footsteps of John Muir, glide on a zip line, enjoy a real Wild West bar in Coulterville, explore the authentic gold rush era town of Mariposa, sip local wine and craft beer, dine on local food, or take in a unique regional event.

www.yosemiteexperience.com

cazenove+loyd

cazenove+loyd are the experts in experiential travel. Started over 20 years ago by Henrietta Loyd, they create tailor-made trips to three exciting and challenging parts of the world, Africa + Indian Ocean, South + South East Asia and Central + South America. They also design a selection of intimate and exclusive small group experiences that offer unprecedented private access to some of the world's most inspiring places and cultures. Extraordinary experiences for every client.

www.cazloyd.com

Adobe

The Adobe® Photoshop® family of products is the ultimate playground for bringing out the best in your digital images, transforming them into anything you can imagine, and showcasing them in extraordinary ways. Manage, develop, print or export your images to the web using Photoshop Lightroom 4 and Adobe Photoshop CS6 for state-of-the-art imaging magic, exciting new creative options, and blazingly fast performance. Retouch with new Content-Aware features, and create superior designs as well as movies, using new and re-imagined tools and workflows.

www.adobe.com   www.adobe.com/products/photoshop/family

FUJiFILM

Condé Nast Traveller

Fujifilm

Fujifilm is a global leader in imaging technology, products and services including digital cameras, photofinishing, digital storage and recording media, consumer and professional film, motion picture film, professional video, printing systems, medical imaging, office technology, flat panel displays and graphic arts. The company employs more than 73,000 people worldwide, with 178 subsidiaries stretching across four continents. In the UK, Fujifilm has been supplying the imaging, printing and graphics industries, as well as consumers, professional and enthusiast photographers, with high quality, innovative products and services for over 25 years. All the TPOTY exhibition prints are produced on Fujifilm Crystal Archive paper and Direct to Media.

www.fujifilm.eu/uk

Condé Nast Traveller

Condé Nast Traveller is the world's most discerning travel title. Appealing to both men and women, it provides authoritative, useful and independent features not only on destinations, but also on world issues likely to affect the passionate traveller. The US edition has received six National Magazine Awards, the highest honour in magazine publishing, while the UK edition has won numerous accolades, including the PPA Consumer Lifestyle Magazine of the Year on two occasions.

www.cntraveller.com

SPONSORS AND PARTNERS

Explore

Explore has been offering small-group adventure holidays to the world's most exciting destinations for over 30 years. You can now enjoy over 400 trips in more than 130 countries, including adult discovery tours, family adventures, short breaks, wildlife, cycling and trekking trips. Explore has two sister brands: Explore Tailormade, which offers customised, tailor-made travel for all budgets; and Edge, off-beat, interactive and excellent value small-group trips for 18 to 39 year-olds.

www.explore.co.uk   www.explore.co.uk/tailormade   www.edgeadventures.com

Photo Iconic

Photo Iconic offers a range of TPOTY photography courses, workshops and masterclasses to suit all abilities and styles of photography, all tutored by award-winning photographers. These range from half-day workshops to one-week courses and include the festival of photography - Travel Photography Live - in association with Travel Photographer of the Year (TPOTY). Photo Iconic also runs the TPOTY Photo Tours; a selection of photographic holidays and adventures to some of the world's most interesting and inspiring destinations.

www.photoiconic.com.

Tribes Travel

Since 1998 Tribes Travel has been offering seriously special tailor-made wildlife, nature and cultural holidays. They organise inspiring experiences such as spotting jaguars in Brazil, or wild dogs in Botswana; hiking Peru's Inca Trail, or Nepal's Himalayas; taking African safaris by jeep, boat, horse or on foot; and exploring the cities and cultures of India or Morocco. Travel is all about the experiences we have and the incredible insights and memories we build for ourselves. For most of us, photography is key to this which is why Tribes Travel is delighted to be sponsoring the Travel Photographer of the Year.

www.tribes.co.uk

Digimarc

Digimarc is a leading technology provider based in Beaverton, Oregon (USA). Digimarc enables businesses and governments worldwide to identify all forms of content, including audio, video and imagery using imperceptible, persistent digital watermarks embedded into your images © communicating ownership and other information wherever the images travel across the internet. Whether you're a novice photographer or seasoned professional, we have several editions to meet your needs.

www.digimarc.com

Plastic Sandwich

Plastic Sandwich has been putting together portfolios for photographers and art directors since the early 1970s. It was founded, and is still run, by Joyce Pinto and Rob Jacobs - who has been with the company for over 30 years. Between them they have unparalleled experience in the field of image presentation in its various forms over the last 40 years and have been the proud sponsors of the TPOTY competition since 2003. Plastic Sandwich's services are also utilised by companies such as event and PR organisations, film companies, high-end presenters, and anyone whose activities or craft are best shown through the presentation of images. We are now direct suppliers to Jaguar Land Rover.

www.plasticsandwich.co.uk

Radisson Blu Edwardian London

A collection of individual hotels in great London, Guildford and Manchester locations, Radisson Blu Edwardian Hotels range from bijou boutique to large-scale luxe. Think contemporary design that doesn't compromise on comfort, complimentary wi-fi throughout and great seasonal British food, with service that anticipates but never assumes. It's an experience that relaxes and stimulates in equal measure. Situated in the heart of the Mayfair village, the May Fair Hotel has become a by-word for elegance and style. Once owned by film impresarios the Danziger Brothers, the hotel has a unique pedigree built upon a heritage of film, art, music and fashion.

www.radissonblu-edwardian.com   www.themayfairhotel.co.uk

Rome, Italy. **Tom McLaughlan, UK.**

SPONSORS AND PARTNERS

Royal Geographical Society
with IBG

Advancing geography
and geographical learning

Royal Geographical Society (with IBG)

The Royal Geographical Society (with The Institute of British Geographers) was formed in 1830 for 'the advancement of geographical science'. Today, they deliver this objective by developing, supporting and promoting geography through research, expeditions and fieldwork, education, and public engagement, while also providing geographical input to policy. They hold the world's largest private geographical collection and provide public access to it. In 2011 the Society embarked on a five-year partnership with Travel Photographer of the Year to host major annual exhibitions of the awards' stunning travel photography, supported by an ongoing programme of workshops and events.

www.rgs.org

Young Photographers' Alliance

The Young Photographers' Alliance (YPA) was created to help young photographers, aged between 18 and 29, bridge the gap between their passion for photography and professional success. While digital technology has made the mechanics of taking pictures easier, the industry itself, already complex and competitive, is becoming ever harder to break into. Initially founded in New York in 2009, YPA is now established here in the UK. Led by industry professionals, YPA nurtures young talent, helping them to develop both the photographic skills and business acumen required to build successful and sustainable careers, providing access to practical industry knowledge, resources and contacts.

www.ypauk.org

SPONSORS AND PARTNERS

Genesis Imaging

One of the UK's leading photographic image printers, Genesis Imaging is in the unique position of offering all manner of photographic printing, mounting and framing services for the creative industry. They believe photographic printing is an art. They print images of the highest calibre for some of the best-known professional photographers, artists and art galleries around – people who demand the very best quality available. Their superb Giclée Fine Art and Lambda prints have graced the walls of numerous famous galleries, from London's National Portrait Gallery to New York's Museum of Modern Art. Genesis Imaging print and mount all the Travel Photographer of the Year exhibitions.

www.genesisimaging.co.uk

iriδius

Iridius

Iridius offers a wide range of design and training services to a growing list of clients, including Adobe, Hewlett Packard, Royal Doulton, Porsche, Audi, Transco, Warner Lambert, Top Yachts, MEM Consumer Finance, Harper Collins, Streamline, Faversham House Group, Travel Photographer of the Year and numerous small to medium enterprises. Although they are a small team, they use this to their advantage: they don't have administration and management overheads and they work quickly and efficiently. Iridius design the Travel Photographer of the Year "Journey" portfolio books and website.

www.iridius.co.uk

Connekt Colour

Founded in 1991, Connekt Colour has 20 years of colour and colour reproduction experience. Their impressive portfolio of longstanding clients is testimony to their consistent levels of quality and service. They view themselves very much as an extension of you and your clients' business and are always keen to be involved from the start of a project, offering advice and solutions to get a better job or save you money. In 2009 they were awarded Best Digital Book of The Year at the British Book Design and Production Awards and in 2010 their digital partner, Litho Division, won Best Photographic Art/Architecture Monograph Book. Connekt Colour prints all the Travel Photographer of the Year portfolio books and cards.

www.connektcolour.com

Direct Photographic

With offices in London, Paris and Cape Town, Direct Photographic is dedicated to delivering the very best in rental equipment to photographers Worldwide. An active supporter of the industry as a whole, Direct Photographic is a keen investor in the latest equipment and remains committed to helping capture the vision of both emerging and established photographers.With an extensive range of products, including the latest in HD camera and LED lighting technology, plus continual investment throughout every aspect of its business, Direct Photographic is the perfect choice for every photographic project. Direct Photographic light the Travel Photographer of the Year exhibition at the Royal Geographical Society (with IBG) in London.

www.directphotographic.co.uk